W9-BYW-309

The Girl's Guide to
FAIRIES

Everything Irresistible
about the Fair Folk

by Sheri A. Johnson

CAPSTONE PRESS
a capstone imprint

Snap Books are published by Capstone Press,
151 Good Counsel Drive, P.O. Box 669, Mankato, Minnesota 56002.
www.capstonepub.com

 Books published by Capstone Press are manufactured with paper
containing at least 10 percent post-consumer waste.

Library of Congress Cataloging-in-Publication Data
Johnson, Sheri.
  The girl's guide to fairies : everything irresistible about the fair folk / by Sheri A. Johnson.
    p. cm. — (Snap. Girls' guides to everything unexplained)
  Includes bibliographical references and index.
  Summary: "Describes the mystery, cool characteristics, and allure of fairies, including historical and
contemporary examples"—Provided by publisher.
  ISBN 978-1-4296-6556-8 (library binding)
  1. Fairies—Juvenile literature. I. Title. II. Series.

  BF1552.J64 2012
  398.21—dc22   2011002452

Editorial Credits
Editor: Mari Bolte
Designer: Tracy Davies
Media Researcher: Svetlana Zhurkin
Production Specialist: Laura Manthe

Photo Credits:
Alamy: AF Archive, 14, Amoret Tanner, 9 (top), Beryl Peters Collection, 22, Lebrecht Music and Arts
Photo Library, 13 (top), Pictorial Press, 29 (top), Stan Rohrer, 21 (top); Cover of "Artemis Fowl: the
Graphic Novel" by Eoin Colfer and Andrew Donkin, art by Giovanni Rigano, color by Paolo Lamanna, 29
(bottom); Dreamstime: Algol, 15, 17 (top), Franciscah, 7, 9 (middle), Leeloomultipass, 10, Maryna Halton,
cover (forest), 23, Rashevskaya, 8; Getty Images: The Bridgeman Art Library/William Holmes Sullivan,
21 (bottom), SSPL, 13 (bottom); iStockphoto: backhanding, cover (sunbeams), Oksana Tsepurnaja,
cover (flying fairies), Patricia Legg, 4 and throughout (wings design element); Library of Congress, 11;
Newscom: Album/New Line Cinema/The Saul Zaentz Company/Wingnut Films, 27 (right), Album/New
Line Productions/Alan Markfield, 28 (bottom), Courtesy of ILM, 28 (top), HO/KRT, 17 (bottom), Scripps
Howard Photo Service, 27 (middle), ZUMA Press/Christian Langbehn, 27 (left); Shutterstock: Algol, cover
(fairy's wings), Brian Chase, 6, Els Jooren, 16 (top), greglith, cover (fairy silhouette), Hannamariah, 20,
Jan Matoska, 18, Liliya Kulianionak, 5, Linda Bucklin, 16 (bottom), Twisted Shots, 9 (bottom); Svetlana
Zhurkin, 19, 29 (middle)

Printed in the United States of America in North Mankato, Minnesota.
032011
006110CGF11

Contents

Chapter One

Merry Fairy or Scary Fairy?

Imagine walking alone at midnight through a forest. You see a glimmer of light out of the corner of your eye. You turn just in time to catch a flash of delicate wings in the moonlight. Then it's gone.

What did you see? Was it someone playing a trick?

Could it have been a lightning bug? A moth? Or was it something supernatural? Could you have seen a fairy?

Just what is a fairy? The word "fairy" comes from the Latin word *fata*, or spirit. You may have seen it spelled "faerie"—that's the Old French spelling.

Fairies are sometimes seen as tiny, ageless beauties with wings. But other creatures fall under the category of fairy too. Elves, pixies, gnomes, and brownies are just a few types of fairies. Goblins, gremlins, trolls, and ogres are some of the nastier creatures in the fairy family.

There is more to fairies than meets the eye.

Most of us have heard about the Tooth Fairy. Disney made Tinkerbell and her friends famous. In the Legend of Zelda video game series, fairies can heal injuries. But not all fairies are so nice.

Fairies have appeared in stories all over the world.

Fairies have human appearances but are mythical creatures. They all have some kind of mysterious magical power. But they come in different types, sizes, colors, and personalities. So are fairies sweet and **mischievous** or scary and mean?

mischievous: able or tending to cause trouble in a playful way

Fairies are born fairies. You can't become one. So where do fairies come from? What are they? Are they real?

Some people say that fairies don't exist. But stories about fairies have been around since ancient times. One popular belief was that fairies were ghosts or the spirits of dead people. Another theory claimed them to be intelligent aliens. Still others believed that fairies were related to humans but evolved in a new way. Some cultures believed fairies to be demons or fallen angels. In Ireland fairies were treated as mythical gods and goddesses. Flitter through these pages to learn more about these spirited sprites.

Chapter Two

Fairy Features

Fairies have changed throughout history. Long ago, people described fairies as tall and elegant. Over time, they shrunk and gained wings. Stories and movies have changed our **perception** of fairies. To make matters more complicated, different types of fairies have different behaviors and looks.

perception : how we see or understand things

Behavior: All fairies have one thing in common—they are **unpredictable**! Sometimes good fairies are naughty, and bad fairies are kind. A kind fairy mother may be unhappy with her sickly fairy baby. She might then steal a human baby. Or a nasty fairy may decide to help a homeowner with chores.

Fairies love to play tricks on humans, play music, and dance. But fairies are very sensitive when people talk about them. Harmful pranks happen to humans who gossip about fairy folk.

Looks: All fairies have pointed ears. But their bodies come in different shapes and sizes. Some fairies are tiny and pretty with delicate wings. Others are tall and graceful, like the elves in The Lord of the Rings books. The fairies, doxies, and pixies in the Harry Potter series are small and fierce.

Clothing: Fairies are fussy about their fashions, but styles vary by type. Elves enjoy beautiful white silk and expensive clothes. Brownies wear wrinkled rags. Gnomes show off green coats and red caps. Leprechauns sport formal attire including jackets, stockings, and hats. Of course, some fairies prefer to go naked or simply wear leaves and moss.

unpredictable: not knowing what will happen in the future

There are other ways to identify a fairy. Their ears and clothing aren't the only giveaways!

Their ability to do magic is what really reveals them as supernatural.

Magical Powers: Fairies have a wealth of powers and abilities. These skills include shape-shifting, flying, **teleporting**, and invisibility. Their magical powers even extend to their lifespans. Some fairies have been reported as **immortal**, but most live between 400 and 1,000 years.

teleport: to transport oneself by instantly disappearing from one location and reappearing in another

Home: It's been said that fairies live in an enchanted place known as Fairyland. But where is Fairyland? No one knows for sure. It could be inside hollow hills or trees or under waterfalls. Some think it's in a different dimension or a parallel world.

Few visitors have been lucky enough to visit Fairyland and return. Be warned! Legend says that eating fairy food can trap you in Fairyland forever. And watch the time. What seems like a few hours there can equal a few years in our time.

Fairies dancing in Fairyland

immortal: able to live forever

Chapter Three

Mingling with Mortals

Are you sure your best friend is human? He or she could be a fairy in disguise! According to stories and legends, fairies hang out in the human world all the time.

These fairies could be on a quest to help a human hero on an adventure. They could be sent by the rulers of Fairyland as spies or messengers. Or they could be looking for fun. Fairies looking for human partners use glamour. This magic is used to trick humans into entering Fairyland.

The worst reason fairies come into our world is to steal human babies! Fairy parents often envy a human's plump, healthy infant. Sometimes they will kidnap the baby to raise as their own. They will leave a replacement, called a changeling, in its place.

The changeling could be a sick fairy baby or an old fairy wanting to be cuddled. Even a piece of wood could be **enchanted** to look like a baby. It's easy to spot a changeling if you know what you're looking for. Bad temper? Sickly-looking? Messy hair? Loves to eat? You may have a changeling!

Fairies appear all over the world but rarely leave traces of their existence. But there are some signs that fairies are real. In 1917 cousins Frances Griffiths and Elsie Wright took five photographs of themselves with fairies. The fairies were called the Cottingley fairies, after the place in England where the pictures were taken.

More than 60 years later, the girls admitted the pictures were fake—except for one! Frances claimed to the end that they had seen fairies. She said that the one picture was real.

Elsie Wright and a fairy

enchant: to put under the spell of magic

Chapter Four

Mischief or Malice?

There are all sorts of fairies out there. Whether good or evil, tall or small, beautiful or frightening, there's something fascinating about these supernatural creatures. What kind of fairy would you want to be? There are many types to choose from!

Elves are the most humanlike of all fairies. They are tall, beautiful, strong, and brave warriors. They live together in elf communities and have their own languages.

Elves are talented musicians and the keepers of the forest. Some can even see into the future. You can find these talented and gorgeous elves in The Lord of the Rings or in the Shannara series.

But not all elves are mysterious fighters. Harry Potter's helpful house elves, Dobby and Kreacher, are short with long ears and noses. Even Santa has elves. His cute creatures wear stocking hats and spend their days making toys. Christmas elves started appearing alongside St. Nick in the 1800s.

Brownies are the best-known household fairies. Small, shaggy, and brown, they are about half the size of a normal human. They adopt a family and pitch in with unfinished chores while the humans are asleep. Brownies like to be paid with a bowl of cream or honey. If they receive a gift they don't like, they will leave.

Boggarts are the nasty opposites of Brownies. Ragged and hairy, these angry creatures bring misfortune wherever they go. Boggarts like to hide things, pull peoples' ears, ring the phone at odd hours, and rearrange furniture. Any Harry Potter fan will recall that these shape-shifters are tough to get rid of!

Dwarfs are older looking with short, stocky, and strong bodies. They often sport long beards. They live in underground caves and work in mines where they turn precious metals into objects with magical powers. The dwarfs in the game *World of Warcraft* are brave fighters with hot tempers and a love for treasure.

Leprechauns are Ireland's version of fairies. These creatures wear red or green and first appeared in a tale from the Middle Ages. Short and squat, leprechauns often look like old men. They are best known for guarding their pots of gold and tricking humans. Anyone who finds a leprechaun's pot of gold is said to win three wishes.

Gremlins are naughty critters that are hard on electronics. They love messing with electrical appliances and machinery. During World War II (1939–1945), pilots often blamed unexplained equipment trouble on these rascally critters.

Pixies are the most beloved of fairy folk. They like to wear green. Pixies are no larger than a hand, but they can shape-shift to any size. They have **translucent** wings, oversized heads, and pointed ears and noses. Pixies are practical jokers. Their favorite prank is to make humans lose their way. To counter being "pixie-led," turn your clothes inside out.

Giants and Ogres are very large creatures known for being mean and nasty. Hagrid, Harry Potter's half-giant friend, challenges this belief. Other giants in the magical world are not so nice.

Gnomes are known for being kind, jolly, and clever. They are short, usually about 2 feet (0.6 meters) tall, and can live for thousands of years. Gnomes are seen as protectors of nature. This is why people today often place ceramic statues of gnomes in their gardens.

translucent: allowing some light to pass through

Goblins are dark, mean-spirited fairies. They are known for being thieves and villains. They live in bands in dark underground places and deep forests. They sometimes make slaves of other fairies. Goblins are seen as companions to the dead, especially near Halloween.

water goblin

Trolls should be avoided at all cost. They are powerful, unpleasant fairies. Some believe they are a cross between dwarfs and giants. Their tough skin and powerful bodies make them fierce fighters. In the Elenium series, trolls are huge creatures who love snacking on human flesh.

Hobgoblins are sometimes confused with regular goblins. But these fairies are closer to their cousins, the brownies. While hobgoblins are rather ugly, these fairies are actually helpful with household chores. Like Harry Potter's house elf friend, Dobby, giving a hobgoblin clothes will allow it to leave your home.

Banshees are female water fairies with long flowing hair. They wail right before someone is about to die. Their eyes are bloodshot from their constant crying. Native to Ireland, banshees have been known to appear to certain families more than others.

FACT

Love trolls? The Troll Museum in New York City is home to hundreds of troll dolls.

CHARMING FAIRIES

Want to find a fairy? Well, fairies choose who sees them, but your chances improve when you're surrounded by nature. Try spending time in forests, country places, gardens, and hills.

You could find a fairy in your own backyard!

Narrow trails, called fairy paths, are signs there are fairies in the area. Keep your eyes open for rings of mushrooms, known as fairy rings. Fairies love using fairy rings for dancing. One of the largest fairy rings ever found was in France. It was 2,000 feet (610 meters) in diameter and more than 700 years old! It's good luck to find a fairy ring. But those who step into fairy rings may be forced to dance nonstop until sunrise.

Certain times are better than others when it comes to spotting a fairy. The best days are May Day, Midsummer's Eve (a day between June 21–24), and Halloween. The best time of day is during the change between light and dark, such as dawn and dusk. You are also more likely to find fairies dancing, singing, and partying at midnight during a full moon.

Since fairies choose who they will reveal themselves to, it is important to be on your best behavior. Be sincere, kind, and respectful. You can also try to bribe a fairy by leaving bread, milk, and honey out at night.

Fairy pranks can be harmful, but there are steps you can take to avoid being tricked. Come home early and stay in all night. Don't accept anything from a fairy, especially food. Don't ever try to harm a fairy. Put on a daisy chain and keep something made of iron nearby.

Wear your clothes turned inside out to avoid or reverse the effects of glamour.

To keep a fairy away, carry oats, a twig from a broom, or a four-leaf clover in your pocket. Keep them out of your house by tying red thread around a doorknob and hanging bells on your doorway.

You can also leave gifts for fairies. Since fairies can find gifts offensive, they may leave. You can scare fairies off with running water, loud noises, and salt. When you go to bed at night, place your shoes nearby. Set them on top of your socks, with the toes of the shoes pointing away from the bed.

There are many ways to keep fairies away.

QUIZ: Find Your Inner Fairy

Now that you know a little bit about fairies, find out if you could be one! This handy quiz will let you know if you fit the fairy profile.

When it comes to size:

a. I am the tallest in class.

b. They call me half-pint.

c. Are you calling me short?

d. It doesn't matter. I can change to any size I want.

You are most relaxed:

a. in the forest.

b. comfy at home.

c. exploring caves.

d. near people.

When it comes to fashion, you prefer:

a. name brand expensive clothes and silky white attire.

b. wrinkled and I'm just fine with that, thank you.

c. comfortable working clothes.

d. anything green.

Your favorite pastime is:

a. making music and dancing.
b. cleaning the house (it could happen …).
c. making jewelry.
d. pulling pranks on people.

 You consider yourself to be:

a. pretty and powerful
b. helpful and secretive
c. skilled and strong
d. fun and lighthearted

 6. When you encounter conflict you:

a. attack
b. disappear from sight
c. stand firm
d. What conflict? Everyone loves me!

Look through your answers to find your true inner fairy. If you have:

Mostly As: You are just missing your pointy ears—you are an elf!

Mostly Bs: You are a helpful critter—what a brownie!

Mostly Cs: Talented and rather touchy—you are a dwarf!

Mostly Ds: Mischievous and playful—you are a pixie!

✦ ✦ ✦ ✦ ✦ ✦ ✦ ✦ ✦ ✦ ✦ ✦ ✦ ✦ ✦ ✦ ✦ ✦

READ, WATCH and LEARN

Want to be in the know about fairies? Then you'll want to be familiar with the classics. In the 16th century, French writer Madame d'Aulnoy used the term "fairy tale" to describe her stories.

The first fairy tales were scarier than what we're used to today. They were designed to teach some sort of lesson. Today fairy tales might not even have fairies in them. Modern fairy tales are usually just fantastic stories that include magic.

READ IT: Artemis Fowl (series) by Eoin Colfer

Artemis Fowl is a teenage criminal mastermind bent on getting rich. In the first book, Artemis is convinced that fairies are real and sets out to capture one. He captures fairy Holly Short. Throughout the series, Holly and Artemis make their way through a variety of settings and situations. With more than 18 million copies sold, this series is a modern-day fairy tale.

READ IT: The Spiderwick Chronicles (series) by Holly Black and Tony DiTerlizzi

Jared, Simon, and Mallory Grace move into the Spiderwick Estate. They discover a hidden library and later a field guide to magical creatures. The Grace children begin their adventures, revealing a world filled with creatures such as brownies, hobgoblins, dwarfs, elves, and goblins.

WATCH IT: The Lord of the Rings trilogy

Hobbit Frodo Baggins finds himself in possession of the One Ring of Power. The Dark Lord, Sauron, needs the ring to conquer the world. Frodo and his eight companions must make the trip toward Mount Doom to destroy the ring and ensure the safety of Middle-earth.

VOTED FAMOUS

Most Helpful
Dobby the House Elf

Although Dobby's help sometimes does Harry Potter more harm than good, Dobby is always loyal. His powers include teleporting, **levitation**, and enchantment.

Biggest Heart
Buddy the Elf

An orphan who crawled into Santa's gift sack, Buddy made the North Pole his home. This man-sized Christmas elf will charm you as he fights for his family and for the Christmas spirit.

levitation : to rise in the air and float

Beautiful Bowman
Legolas

With his long blond locks and wicked bow-and-arrow skills, Legolas has shot to the top as one of the most popular Lord of the Rings characters.

Sparkling Sidekick
Navi the Fairy

Link needs all the help he can get in *The Legend of Zelda: The Ocarina of Time*. Navi is at his side as they try to save Hyrule from the evil Ganandorf.

Law Enforcer
Holly Short

Artemis Fowl's foe and friend, Holly is the only female officer in the LEPrechon squad. She's not above breaking the rules to help her friends or lay down the law.

GLOSSARY

enchant (en-CHANT)—to put under the spell of magic

immortal (i-MOR-tuhl)—able to live forever

levitate (LEV-i-tate)—to rise in the air and float

mischievous (MISS-chuh-vuhss)—able or tending to cause trouble in a playful way

perception (per-SEP-shuhn)—how we see or understand things

supernatural (soo-pur-NACH-ur-uhl)—something that cannot be given an ordinary explanation

teleport (TELL-uh-port)—to transport oneself by instantly disappearing from one location and reappearing in another

translucent (trans-LOO-suhnt)—allowing some light to pass through

unpredictable (un-pri-DIK-tuh-buhl)—not knowing what will happen in the future

READ MORE

Despeyroux, Denise, and abridged and adapted by Alissa Heyman. *The Big Book of Fairies*. New York: Sterling, 2010.

Knudsen, Shannon. *Fairies and Elves*. Fantasy Chronicles. Minneapolis, Minn.: Lerner, 2010.

Niehaus, Alisha, and Shannon Beatty, ed. *Fairypedia*. New York: DK Publishing, 2009.

INTERNET SITES

FactHound offers a safe, fun way to find Internet sites related to this book. All of the sites on FactHound have been researched by our staff.

Here's all you do:

Visit *www.facthound.com*

Type in this code: 9781429665568

 Super-cool stuff! Check out projects, games and lots more at **www.capstonekids.com**

INDEX